Verona
Travel Guide

Quick Trips Series

No part of this publication may be reproduced, stored in a retrieval system, or transmitted, in any form or by any means without the prior written permission of the publisher, nor be otherwise circulated in any form of binding or cover other than that in which it is published and without similar condition being imposed on the subsequent purchaser. If there are any errors or omissions in copyright acknowledgements the publisher will be pleased to insert the appropriate acknowledgement in any subsequent printing of this publication. Although we have taken all reasonable care in researching this book we make no warranty about the accuracy or completeness of its content and disclaim all liability arising from its use.

Copyright © 2016, Astute Press
All Rights Reserved.

Table of Contents

VERONA ... 6

- CUSTOMS & CULTURE ... 8
- GEOGRAPHY ... 11
- WEATHER & BEST TIME TO VISIT ... 14

SIGHTS & ACTIVITIES: WHAT TO SEE & DO ... 16

- RECOMMENDED ITINERARIES ... 17
  - One Day in Verona ... 17
  - Two Days in Verona ... 19
- HISTORIC MONUMENTS ... 20
  - Piazza Bra ... 20
  - Juliet's House ... 23
  - Romeo's House ... 24
  - Piazza Erbe ... 25
- HOLY PLACES & CHURCHES ... 26
  - Cathedral of Verona in Duomo ... 26
  - Basilica of San Zeno ... 28
  - San Giorgio in Braida Church ... 28
- CASTLES & FORTRESSES ... 29
  - Castelvecchio ... 29
  - San Pietro Castle ... 30
  - Scaligeri Castle ... 31
- WELLNESS ACTIVITIES & NATURE ... 31

    South Adige Park 31
    North Adige Park 32
    Giusti Palace & Garden 32
    Regional Natural Park of Lessinia 33
    Thermal Resorts 33

☯ Amusement Parks & Other Attractions 34

    Gardaland Resort 34
    Beaches 36
    Parco Naturo Viva 37

BUDGET TIPS   39

☯ Accommodation 39

    Hotel Europa 39
    Hotel San Luca 40
    Hotel Siena 40
    Hotel Mastino 41
    Hotel Marco Polo 42

☯ Places to Eat 43

    Antica Bottego del Vino 43
    Trattoria Il Pompiere 44
    Il Desco 44
    Maharajah 45
    Locanda Castelvecchio 46

☯ Shopping 47

    Federica Casanova 47
    Baol atelier Creativo 47
    Spazio Espoitivo Memoire 48
    Citta del Sole 48
    Via Mazzini 48

KNOW BEFORE YOU GO   50

☯ Entry Requirements 50
☯ Health Insurance 50
☯ Travelling with Pets 51

- 🌐 Airports 51
- 🌐 Airlines 53
- 🌐 Currency 54
- 🌐 Banking & ATMs 54
- 🌐 Credit Cards 54
- 🌐 Tourist Taxes 55
- 🌐 Reclaiming VAT 55
- 🌐 Tipping Policy 56
- 🌐 Mobile Phones 56
- 🌐 Dialling Code 57
- 🌐 Emergency Numbers 57
- 🌐 Public Holidays 58
- 🌐 Time Zone 58
- 🌐 Daylight Savings Time 59
- 🌐 School Holidays 59
- 🌐 Trading Hours 59
- 🌐 Driving Laws 60
- 🌐 Drinking Laws 61
- 🌐 Smoking Laws 61
- 🌐 Electricity 62
- 🌐 Tourist Information (TI) 62
- 🌐 Food & Drink 63
- 🌐 Websites 64

VERONA TRAVEL GUIDE

Verona

Located midway between Venice and Milan in Northern Italy is the historic and picturesque city of Verona. Verona's claim to fame is as the setting for the greatest love story ever written – Shakespeare's Romeo and Juliet. Listed as a UNESCO World Heritage Site, Verona impresses visitors with its Roman ruins, medieval charm, and cultural heritage. The city is cradled along the curves of the River Adige, which, coupled with the backdrop of the cypress-covered hills creates a visual treat.

Although the origin of the city and name is unknown, it is at least 2000 years old. Verona was founded as a political and commercial town by the Romans, traces of which can be seen today in the architecture and ruins sprinkled all across the city.

Verona was the intersection of many major medieval routes making it a point of interest and prized possession of many kingdoms. Over the centuries it came under the regime of many great rulers including Theoderic the Great, Charlemagne, Emperor Maximilian I, and Napoleon. Its importance for its strategic location remained even after the days of the World War II.

VERONA TRAVEL GUIDE

During these medieval centuries of political strife and battles, Verona continuously grew as a city of art and culture. It was the setting of 2 major works of Shakespeare – Romeo and Juliet and the Two Gentlemen of Verona. Present day Verona celebrates art and culture through opera, theater, art exhibitions, and a variety of festivals and events throughout the year. For those who are looking for a slice of nature - the surrounding areas of Verona are excellent for a hike or a drive. Considering the size of the city, Verona is a shopaholic's delight. From traditional crafts to major global brands, the range is wide and attractive.

Although Verona does not attract as many visitors as neighboring Venice and Milan, it is actually a boon for those who travel here.

VERONA TRAVEL GUIDE

Tourists can enjoy a relaxing visit in this city, together with an authentic 'taste and feel' of Italy. Its proximity to major tourist cities means that it is also ideal for a 1-day or 2-day trip from Venice and Milan. Verona is able to entertain tourists of all ages and interest through its ancient ruins, family theme parks, vibrant nightlife, culinary delights, and a host of events and festivals.

🌐 Customs & Culture

The city of Verona is a melting pot of ancient culture and contemporary lifestyle. From lovers of classical music and art to the new age hip hop and rock concerts, Verona has all on offer. The city is home to the oldest music academy in the world. The ancient Roman Arena is still a venue to many cultural events and festivals and has attracted some of the world's foremost artists in the recent past. With so

VERONA TRAVEL GUIDE

much going on throughout the year, there is never a moment of boredom in Verona.

Tourists visiting Verona between July and August should not miss the opera season. This is an opportunity to watch open-air opera and performances in one of the largest ancient Roman amphitheaters in the world – the 1st century Arena de Verona. Once the stage for gladiator fights, the arena transforms itself to the venue for many popular operas like Madam Butterfly and Carmen. Around the same time the Roman Theater at the other end of the city also comes to life with Shakespearean plays and the Verona Jazz Festival.

Carnival lovers are in for a treat in Verona. First started in 1615, the Annual Carnival of Verona is one of the biggest events in the city. Held on Fat Tuesday, the city gets into

VERONA TRAVEL GUIDE

a party mood with over 500 floats in the parade and over 15000 kilos of sweets and candies tossed into the crowd! One of the highlights during the carnival is the night parade - Carnevale di notte a Monteforte – on the last Saturday of the festivities. Masked participants and floats parade through the city streets amidst much fanfare.

On the first Sunday every July the city gears up for another popular festival - Festa del Cimbri a Camposilvano. During the whole day the city is drowned in parades, feasting, religious rites, and shooting trombonis – a kind of traditional hook gun or harquebus. The day ends with the crowning of the King of the Cimbri.

Romance and Verona go hand in hand. The 'Schermi d'Amore Festival del Cinema Sentimentale' is an annual film festival (end of March) focusing only on romantic

VERONA TRAVEL GUIDE

films. The Verona Film Festival every April that follows has a wider variety of feature films from all over the world. The summer months also has a number of pop and rock concerts including the Festivalbar that attracts many international artists. Similarly the winter months have the Teatro Nuevo and the Teatro Filarmonico.

A discussion on Verona cannot be complete without the mention of the Verona wine. Regarded as one the best in Italy, the city has been very protective of the tradition and the making of this wine.

It is home to one of the most prestigious wine festivals in the world – the Vinitaly - http://www.vinitaly.com/EN. Started in 1967, this 5 day festival today attracts thousands of wine lovers from many parts of the world. It is not only a wine tasting festival but a business opportunity for many. Those visiting Verona in early September (2nd Sunday) can enjoy the wine tasting through the Festa dell'Ulva – the grape festival. Other than wine tasting, the festival also features a grape-crushing contest.

🌍 Geography

Verona is located in the Vento region in northern Italy and is the 3rd largest city in that region, after Venice and Milan. Major cities close to Verona include Venice (105 km), Bologna (109 km), Milan (140 km), Florence (186 km), and Genoa (198 km). The city is well connected with Italy and the rest of Europe through air, road, and rail service.

Located about 12 km from the city center, Verona is served by the Catullo Airport, IATA – VRN - http://www.aeroportoverona.it/en/passeggeri_t5/. The airport was remodeled in 2006 and has all the modern amenities. It has a number of low cost and regular carriers including Easyjet, Trawelfly, Wizzair, British Airways, and Lufthansa, to name a few.

Direct connections are available with many domestic and international cities that include Rome, Catania Fontanarossa, London, Amsterdam, and Moscow. The airport has an aerobus (€6) that connects it to the train station that has direct connections to the city center. For those who want a more comfortable ride can opt for the taxi outside the Arrival section.

Those arriving by train will enter the city through the Verona Porta Nuova Station. Regular connections are available with a number of cities through high-speed trains as well as the slower and cheaper regional express

VERONA TRAVEL GUIDE

trains. The high speed train from Milan takes about 1 hr 25 min and costs €21 whereas the slower Regional Express takes just a shade less than 2 hrs and costs €11. Other than Milan, there are direct connections with Venice, Rome, Padua, and Bologna.

Verona is connected by the A4 and A22 motorway. There are regular international bus connections like Eurolines which connect the city with the rest of Europe. For those driving in, it will be a very scenic drive from both Milan and Venice.

Once in the city, visitors can choose the public bus service run by ATV - http://www.atv.verona.it/flex/cm/pages/ServeBLOB.php/L/EN/IDPagina/1?53fdc478483c1. Taxis and rental cars are also available through a number of operators.

VERONA TRAVEL GUIDE

Verona is a bike-friendly city where visitors can rent a bike on a daily, weekly, or monthly basis. Those planning to drive in Verona should note that the historic city center is a no-auto zone except for the residents and those staying in the hotels. Parking often becomes a cause of delay during the tourist season so visitors should account for that time in advance.

Weather & Best Time to Visit

Although influenced by the Mediterranean-type climate of neighboring Lake Garda, Verona has a typical humid subtropical climate with warm summers and cold to very cold winters. The warmer months (between April and September) have an average high of around 21 degrees Celsius and an average low around 15 degrees. In the colder months (between Oct and March) temperatures

VERONA TRAVEL GUIDE

reach a high of around 5 degrees Celsius and often plunge to a low below freezing point – minus 1 to 2 degrees. Humidity is high but precipitation is low throughout the year with even the wettest month having less than 3.5 inches of rain. With sunny days and a pleasant weather during the summer, Verona is best visited between April and October.

VERONA TRAVEL GUIDE

Sights & Activities: What to See & Do

The city of Verona has a number of discount cards aimed at tourists. One of the most popular and recommended is the Verona Card - http://www.tourism.verona.it/en/information/travel-your-way/verona-card. The card allows one free entry to 15 major attractions in the city and discounted entry to another 6. It also allows free rides on the city public buses. The card comes in 2 denominations – 24 hrs (€15) and 72 hrs (€20). This card can be bought from the

VERONA TRAVEL GUIDE

Tourist Information Offices. The Welcome Card and Welcome Fun Card are 2 other tourist cards for those who are planning to stay overnight in Verona. These cards are available from the hotel front desks only. While the Welcome Card brings in discounts in museums, stores, and numerous restaurants and cafes, the Welcome Fun Card is for discounts at the amusement parks. Both the cards allow discounted travel on city public buses.

🌎 Recommended Itineraries

One Day in Verona

Verona's proximity to Venice has made it a popular day trip destination for many tourists. Trains run every 30 minutes throughout the day between the Venice Mestre Station and the Verona Porta Nuova Station. The high speed White Arrow trains (€23) take less than an hour whereas the comparatively slower Regional Express

VERONA TRAVEL GUIDE

trains (€7.50) take about 2 hrs. The Verona train station has a tourist information office where one can pick a tourist map and then set out on foot to see the attractions.

The largest and the most popular square in Verona, Piazza Bra, is a 15-minute walk from the station. It is home to the ancient Roman amphitheater – Verona Arena, the most visited attraction in the city. Also in the same square are the Gran Guardia Palace and the Barbieri Palace – the new town hall of Verona. The square is lined with historic houses, many of which house restaurants and cafes. From the Piazza Bra, a short walk along via Mazzini – a popular shopping street - will lead right up to the Piazza delle Erbe, another popular tourist attraction of the city.

VERONA TRAVEL GUIDE

On the way there are the Santa Maria Church and the historic Teatro Nuovo. The Piazza delle Erbe is like a treasure chest from the medieval era. Baroque architecture, statues, and an ancient fountain make up this beautiful square. This is also a good place to have a relaxed lunch with numerous eateries lined up along the square and its adjoining streets.

After lunch, nothing beats a leisurely walk along the banks of the Adige, which is less than half a km from the square. Located close to the bank is the Verona Cathedral which is a must see when visiting this city. This would take up the most part of the day. Instead of walking back, it is best to take a cab back to the Piazza Bra and then take a short stroll to another major attraction of Verona - Ms Capulet's House or more famously Juliet's House! With the day coming to an end, it is now time to head back to the railway station but not before buying some souvenirs. The streets leading up to the station have a number of souvenir stores, especially near the Arena where one can buy a variety of souvenirs, from traditional products to Verona shot glasses. For those planning to stay back late and have a taste of the Verona nightlife can visit the bars and cafes at Piazza Erbe. Specially recommended is Caffe Filippini.

Two Days in Verona

Those having a second day in Verona can enjoy a different side of the city. The best way to start is to take a cab or a rental car to the neighboring Valpolicella Winery – about 14 km from the Piazza Bra.

On the way back ask the driver to drive up to the hilltop Santa Maria Sanctuary to take a breathtaking view of the

VERONA TRAVEL GUIDE

city. This is one of the most scenic drives in Verona. On the way down you can see the Roman Bridge, the Roman Walls, and the Roman Theater.

Get down at Castelvecchio to admire the medieval castle and the museum. After lunch head to the San Zeno Basilica. The late afternoon and early evening can be spent walking the narrow streets of Verona or relaxing at the public garden just across the bridge. Art lovers can head to the Pinacoteca Museum. If you are visiting in the summer months, check for performances at the Arena or at any of the historic theaters in town.

Historic Monuments

Piazza Bra

This is the largest square in Verona and one of the largest and most-visited in Italy. The square is famous for the

VERONA TRAVEL GUIDE

Roman Arena, the Gran Guardia Palace and the town hall - Barbieri Palace. It is lined with a number of restaurants and cafes complete with their green or white canopy covers. The entrance to the square is through the Portoni della Bra – the ancient gate. The gate comprises of a pentagonal tower with Romanesque arches. To the left of the gate is the entrance of the Lapidary Inscriptions Museum. Those planning to go the museum can have a bird's eye view of the square from the top-floor of the museum.

The most famous resident of the square is undoubtedly the Roman Arena - a 2000-year old Roman amphitheater that is used as a venue for concerts and festivals. It was built around 30AD and was used as an arena for the fight of the gladiators. A major part of the arena was destroyed in an earthquake in 1117. It remained a mere attraction

VERONA TRAVEL GUIDE

for many centuries. By the 2nd half of the 19th century the arena was rediscovered as a venue for operas for its brilliant acoustics. Since 1913 it has remained the venue for the Verona opera season in the summer months. With a seating capacity of 15000, the Arena attracts over half a million ticket sales annually. In the recent years it has become a popular venue for international rock concerts - http://www.arena.it/en-US/HOMEen.html, attracting some of the biggest names of the industry including Paul McCartney, Pink Floyd, Rod Stewart, Duran Duran, Sting, Alicia Keys, and One Direction, to name just a few.

The grand building with several Romanesque arches located on the southern edge of the square is the Gran Guardia Palace. Construction of the building started in 1610 as a shelter for the troops. However, due to lack of

VERONA TRAVEL GUIDE

funds, it took nearly 250 years to complete. Today it is used for exhibitions, meetings, and conferences.

Located between the Arena and the Gran Guardia is the majestic Barbieri Palace – the town hall of Verona. Built in the mid 19th century and named after its architect, the town hall with its gigantic columns is inspired by the look of ancient Roman temples.

The Lapidary Inscriptions Museum near the entrance of the square is one of the oldest museums in Europe. Opened in 1745, the museum has an impressive collection of epigraphs from many historic periods – Roman, Greek, and Etruscan. The Greek inscriptions from 5BC to around 5AD deserve special mention. The museum is open Tuesday to Sunday from 8:30 am to 2 pm and has an entry fee of €4.50.

VERONA TRAVEL GUIDE

Juliet's House

One of the most famous addresses of Verona is Via Cappello No. 23. This 14th century house is believed to be the house of Juliet Capulet – the tragic heroine of Shakespeare's Rome and Juliet. The house is visited by hundreds of thousands of visitors every year making it a top attraction of the city. The house has a small balcony, popularly known as Juliet's balcony. There is a small courtyard which has a bronze statue of Juliet.

Legend has it that stroking the right breast of the statue brings that person good luck and fortune, especially in love. At the entrance of the building there are numerous letters pasted by lovers believing that it would bring them good luck. Popular as Juliet's Wall, it was restored in the recent past and it has now been decided to allow the letters and notes only on replaceable panels to protect the wall. Visitors are allowed to not only enter the building (€6) but also to climb to the balcony. The inside of the building is decorated with costumes and furnishings from the sets of MGM's famous 1936 movie – Rome and Juliet. It is open every day from 8:30 am to 7:30 pm with reduced hours on Mondays.

Romeo's House

Unfortunately, this is a private property and can only be seen from the outside, but that does not stop tourists from visiting this medieval house. Located in the narrow Via Arche Scaligere, this 13th century house originally belonged to the Montecchi family – Romeo's full name was Romeo Montecchi. The high-walled house almost looks like a mini fortress. On the wall of the house there is a bronze inscription of Romeo riding a horse. Although entry to the house is restricted, visitors can enjoy traditional Veronese cuisine at the restaurant on the ground floor.

Piazza Erbe

Connected with Piazza Bra through the popular via Mazzini is the Piazza delle Erbe or the Market Square. Located close to the river bank, this is one of the popular squares in the city with well-preserved Roman architecture and monuments. Adorning the center of the square is the oldest structure in the square – the Madonna Fountain that was built in 1368. It was constructed with marble from the Roman Forum and the thermal baths in the city. The statue of the Madonna is believed to be older than the actual fountain, sculpted in 380AD. Also in the square is the 13th century Capitello or

VERONA TRAVEL GUIDE

Tribuna where the Lords and Podesta of Verona were proclaimed.

Located on the northern side of the square is the Lamberti Tower, named after the family that started its construction in 1172. The tower rises to a height of 84 m and is multi-chromatic with alternating sections of brick-work and tufa. It also features a late 18th century clock. The tower has 2 bells. The smaller bell, named Marnagona was used to signal work hours and fires while the larger bell, Rengo, was rung to summon citizens during war. Nowadays the bells are rung only for funerals. Visitors are allowed access (€6) to the viewing deck of the tower which has excellent panoramic views of the city. It is open from 8:30 am to 7:30 pm every day.

Other notable buildings in the square include the Judges' Hall near the northern side, the stunning Maffei Palace and the Gardello Tower on the western façade, and the crenellated House of the Merchants on the southern side.

🌍 Holy Places & Churches

Cathedral of Verona in Duomo

Located in Piazza Duomo, this cathedral is one of the most popular attractions in Verona. Built in a Gothic-Renaissance style of architecture, the church welcomes visitors with a stunning façade. It was built in 1117 but has gone through many renovations and expansions over the centuries.

However, the basic floor plan and the look of the cathedral has remained the same unlike its interior which is mostly the renovated look from the 15th century. The church premises include the cloister, the Bishop's House, a museum, and a library. The interior of the church has rich carvings and frescoes from noted Italian artists. The nave and the main chapel are works of art in themselves. The cloister is home to Canonical Museum. The Charter Library instituted in the 17th century has many historic volumes of work from the middle ages relating to religion, law, and science. It is open from 10 am to 5:30 pm with reduced hours on Sundays and winter months. There is an entry fee of €2.50.

Basilica of San Zeno

This Romanesque basilica is one of the many religious buildings that were built after the earthquake of 1117. Apart from its simple but attractive façade and interior, a major attraction of the basilica is that its crypt was the setting of the marriage between Romeo and Juliet. The façade of the church is built with cream-colored tuff and has a huge Gothic-styled rose window called the Wheel of Fortune. It has a large bronze door with 48 panels that is decorated with mythological and religious figures. The bell tower of the church stands at 62 m. It originally had 6 bells, 4 of which are still rung on special occasions. The crypt of the church has the remains of St Zeno, to whom the basilica is dedicated. It is open from 8:30 am to 6 pm with reduced hours on Sundays, festival days, and winter months. There is an entry fee of €2.50.

San Giorgio in Braida Church

Located on the bank of the River Adige, this church is regarded as one of the most beautiful in Italy. With its towering dome, interior décor, and rich treasure of artwork, this is one of the must-see churches in Verona. It was built around the 15th century replacing a Benedictine monastery. Artists whose works are seen in the church include Tintoretto, Domenico, and Farinati. The most famous artwork in the church is the Martyrdom of St George just above the altar. The church has free entry and is open from 7:30 am to 11 am and again from 5 pm to 7 pm.

Other popular churches in Verona include the Santa Maria in Organo Church, San Fermo Maggiore Church, and the St Anastasia Basilica.

🌍 Castles & Fortresses

Castelvecchio

Built in 1354, the Castelvecchio is a spectacular fortress on the bank of the River Adige. It was one of the most important constructions completed by the ruling Scaliger dynasty. This primarily Gothic-styled red-brick fortress has

7 towers, bridge walls, M-shaped merlons, and 4 main buildings.

It has a surrounding ditch which has been dry for many years. It is strategically linked to the historic Scaligeri Bridge across the river. The museum went through major renovations during the 1950s and is today home to the Castelvecchio Museum with a rich collection of medieval paintings, sculptures, ceramics, and weapons. It also has miniature works of gold. The museum is open every day from 8:30 am to 7:30 pm with reduced hours on Mondays. There is an entry fee of €6.

San Pietro Castle

Crowning the hill on the backdrop of Verona, this castle is believed to be the site where the city was founded. Although it is not open to the public, it is worth walking the stairs up the hill just for the stunning views of the city and the river from the top. The stairs start from the Roman Theater. The surroundings of this 15th century castle are the perfect place to enjoy a romantic sunset.

Scaligeri Castle

This is a 13th century castle which has been transformed into a museum and a popular venue for many public and social events. Together with the watch tower, the castle was an important viewpoint during the middle ages. However, with modern warfare and firearms, the castle and the tower lost its importance. List and schedule of the events at the castle can be found at http://www.villafrancavrturismo.it/index.php/eventi.

VERONA TRAVEL GUIDE

🌍 Wellness Activities & Nature

South Adige Park

Stretching from Ca del Bue to Porto San Pancrazio, this is a huge natural reserve which is often referred to as the green lung of Verona. It is home to many species of flora and fauna and is of great interest to students and researchers. The reserve includes a small island formed from the debris of the River Adige. The park has free entry and can be reached by walking or cycling.

North Adige Park

This park is located close to the historic center in the Corte Molon area. The natural reserve stretches for nearly 1 million sq m and is the ideal place for a relaxed stroll or for bicycling. Do not miss the local plants and orchards at the 'brolo'. Visitors can pick a map of the park at the entrance.

Giusti Palace & Garden

Located a short distance to the east of the Verona city center, this is one of the most beautifully landscaped gardens in the region. This late 16th century Italian Renaissance garden is in perfect harmony with the 16th century neo-Classical palace.

Terrace gardens, hedges, and needle-shaped cypresses together with the backdrop of the lush green hillside make it one of the most scenic places in Verona.

VERONA TRAVEL GUIDE

Regional Natural Park of Lessinia

Located to the north of Verona and stretching right up to the border of the Trento region is the Lessinia Park. The park was opened in 1990. It spans over 10000 hectares and reaches an altitude of 1800 m on the Monte Lessini plateau. Not only are the flora and fauna of great interest to many students and researchers, the natural bridges, caves, dolinas, and fossil deposits make it a wonderfully scenic place for a hike. The park can be explored by foot, on bicycle, and on horseback. Within the park boundaries there are 7 theme-based museums highlighting the historical and natural aspects of the region. Visitors planning to visit the park should not miss the Molina waterfalls, the Veja natural bridge, and the Rovere Mille cave.

Thermal Resorts

The surrounding lake areas of Verona have been famous for their thermal baths from the Roman times. Many modern resorts and spas have grown in these regions where visitors can enjoy a relaxing therapy through ancient natural ways. The Lessini region and the area around Monte Baldo are known for their thermal baths.

The Monte Baldo area also has many medicinal herbs. The Villa dei Cedri near the Garda hinterland has thermal baths with excellent modern facilities. Another popular bath is the Giunone in the Caldiero area - http://www.termedigiunone.it/.

Verona also has many facilities for physical activities. The activities range from the more sedate horse riding and golf, to extreme sports like paragliding, diving, rock climbing, mountain biking, and skiing.

🌐 Amusement Parks & Other Attractions

Gardaland Resort

The Gardaland Resort - http://www.gardaland.it/resort/index-en.php is the most popular amusement park in Verona. The resort, covering 445000 sq m, opened in 1975 and has in its boundaries the amusement park, Gardaland Sea-Life, and Gardaland Hotel. With an annual footfall of 3 million, it is ranked as one of the top amusements parks in the world. The park has 32 rides which includes 6 roller coasters.

The park has 8 theme areas namely Castello Merlino, Piazza, Aladino, Pirati, Rio Bravo, Energy, Fantasy

VERONA TRAVEL GUIDE

Kingdom, and Kids Country. The rides are divided into 3 categories – Adventure, Fantasy, and Adrenaline. While Adventure has the tranquil rides like the Colorado Boat and Jungle Rapids, Adrenaline has the most extreme rides like the Blue Tornado, Space Vertigo, and Top Spin. The park is open for special night hours (€16) in the summer months. The park has a number of restaurants, cafes, and bars serving a variety of cuisines and drinks. There is an entry fee of €29 to the amusement park if booked online in advance (7 days).

The Gardaland Sea-Life has 2 aquariums – Turtle Shelter and Kingdom of Sea Lions. It has an entry fee of €10 if tickets are bought online in advance.

The Gardaland Hotel has themed rooms with packages starting from around €100. Special discounted rates are available for guests who go for the whole package of the park, aquarium, and the hotel.

Beaches

The neighboring Lake Garda offers 40 beaches for those who are looking for some relaxing time by the water, especially during the summer months. These Veronese beaches stretch from Malcesine to Peschiera del Garda and include Lido Paina, Campagnola, Marniga, Fornaci, Cappucinni, and la Cavalla, to name a few. Many of these beaches are free and are equipped with free toilets and showers. The more touristy ones have restaurants and cafes with some even having Wi-Fi!

Parco Naturo Viva

This is a zoo that was opened in 1933. Covering 64 hectares, it is located in the hinterland of Lake Garda and

VERONA TRAVEL GUIDE

is a short drive from the Verona city center. Other than the various animals and birds on display, the zoo also doubles up as a research and training center on plants and animals. The zoo is divided into a Fauna Park, an Extinction Park, and a Safari Park. With many rare species of birds and animals, the zoo is ideal for a fun time for the whole family. It is open from 9 am to 5:30 pm. There is an entry fee of €20 for visitors above 13 years of age. Discounts are available for children and groups.

VERONA TRAVEL GUIDE

Budget Tips

🌐 Accommodation

Hotel Europa

Via Roma 8

Verona

Tel: 39 045 594 744

http://www.veronahoteleuropa.com/en/

This 3 star hotel is located just minutes away from the Verona Arena and plenty of other tourist attractions. The main train station is 1 km away. Parking is available and it has a 24 hr front desk and room service. There are non-smoking rooms. It has free Wi-Fi.

VERONA TRAVEL GUIDE

The elegantly decorated ensuite rooms have cable TV, minibar, safe, hairdryer, and AC. Room rates start from €60 and include breakfast.

Hotel San Luca

Vicolo Volto San Luca 8

Verona

Tel: 39 045 591 333

http://www.sanlucahotel.com/en

This is a 3 star hotel located about 200 m from the Piazza Bra and just outside the restricted auto zone. It is a non-smoking property that has been newly renovated. Facilities include parking, shuttle service, 24 hr front desk, room service, and medical service. It has free Wi-Fi. Pets are allowed. There is an onsite bar in the hotel.

The ensuite rooms come with cable TV, heated towel rail, minibar, AC, safe, hairdryer, and complimentary toiletries. Room rates start from €97 and include breakfast.

Hotel Siena

Via Marconi 41

Verona

Tel: 39 045 800 2182

http://www.hotelsiena-verona.it/

This is a 2 star hotel which is just a 10-minute walk from the Piazza Bra and many other attractions of Verona. It is a non smoking property with 24 hr reception and room service. There is a small garden where breakfast is often served in the summer months. The property also has a vending machine and Wi-Fi.

VERONA TRAVEL GUIDE

The spacious and newly renovated ensuite soundproof rooms have cable TV, AC, and courtesy kit. Room rates start from €78.

Hotel Mastino

Cosro Porta Nuova 16, Verona

Tel: 39 045 595 388

http://www.hotelmastino.it/

Housed in a historic building with refurbished modern accommodation, this is a 3 star hotel that is located very close to the Piazza Bra. It has a 24 hr reception, room service, Wi-Fi, non-smoking rooms and family rooms. Parking is available. Pets are allowed. It has an onsite beauty salon and bar.

The ensuite rooms have soundproof windows, cable TV, minibar, AC, hypoallergenic towels, and safe. Room rates start from €95.

Hotel Marco Polo

Via di Sant'Antonio 21, Verona

Tel: 39 045 801 0885

http://www.hotelmarcopoloverona.it/en/

Located in a former convent in the historic center of Verona, this is a 3 star hotel with extremely eye-catching classical décor and furnishings.

Although the hotel is in a quiet street, it is only 250 m away from the Piazza Bra. Facilities of the hotel include room service, travel desk, concierge service, Wi-Fi, and parking. It has an onsite bar and barber shop.

The ensuite rooms have light colored relaxing color themes with wooden flooring. There is cable TV, minibar, telephone, and safe in every room. Room rates start from €105.

Places to Eat

Antica Bottego del Vino

Via Scudo d Francia 3

Verona

Tel: 39 045 800 4535

http://www.bottegavini.it/en

The city of Verona is known for its wine and this restaurant is an ideal place to try the local wine, especially the regional red wine. This multi award winning place has an extensive wine list and is often frequented by celebrities during the opera season. Wine is served both in glass and whole bottle. It also serves a few dishes to accompany the wine that are traditional to the Veronese cuisine.

Trattoria II Pompiere

Vicolo Regina d'Ungheria 5

Verona

Tel: 39 045 803 0537

http://alpompiere.tv/

This is one of the oldest trattorias in Verona having started its operations in the early 1900s. It is a simple inn having a cozy décor with wooden furnishings. The dining room has the cold-cuts corner and the cheese corner. Knowledgeable and helpful staffs are ever-willing to help the guests choose the correct combinations of dishes. It serves typical Veneto cuisine. The salted pork is specially recommended. A full meal costs about €25.

Il Desco

Via Dietro San Sebastiano 7

Verona

Tel: 39 045 595 358

http://www.ristoranteildesco.it/en/index.html

With 2 Michelin stars, this is one of the popular restaurants of not only Verona but the whole of Italy. Set in an old patrician house, the restaurant has an elegant décor that perfectly complements the food. It is obvious that it is slightly expensive considering its top ratings and nationwide fame. Food served is typically Italian with a signature twist by the prized chefs. Starters, fish, and meat dishes are each priced around €40. The vegetarian and pasta dishes are priced between €25-33.

Maharajah

Via Marconi 28/A

Verona

Tel: 39 045 8011 038

http://www.indian-restaurant-maharajah.com/

Having opened its doors in 2004, this is the first restaurant in Verona serving typical North Indian cuisine. It is run by a North Indian couple thus bringing in the authenticity in the dishes served. The restaurant is popular with the locals and visitors alike for its pleasant ambience and delicious food. It serves both vegetarian and non-vegetarian dishes. It also serves the typical and famous Indian tandoor food – oven-grilled meat and bread.

Locanda Castelvecchio

Corso Castelvecchio 21

Verona

Tel: 39 045 803 0097

http://www.ristorantecastelvecchio.com/eng/ristorante-castelvecchio.php

Set in a historic building with a neo-classical décor; this is a restaurant serving Veronese cuisine. The restaurant has 3 separate dining spaces including a verandah which has 30 covers. Dishes include Veneto soup pasta, Risotto with Italian wine, and a variety of beef and chicken dishes. The boiled meat in sauces is specially recommended.

🌐 Shopping

Federica Casanova

Roman mosaics have been famous for centuries and this store - http://www.federicasanova.it/, not only designs and sells mosaics, it also organizes mosaic workshops, some specially designed for the visiting tourists. Owned by Federica – a mosaic artist - after whom it is named, the store is located in via Sabotino. Guests can design their own stuff and take it back with them or by original and unique hand-crafted mosaic jewelry.

Baol atelier Creativo

This is a fashion and accessories store located in Vicolo Stella 9. Italian fashion and designs have been valued an appreciated the world over and visitors can have a taste of the same in this boutique store. Products on sale include jewelry, bags, dresses, scarves, hats, and sweaters.

Spazio Espoitivo Memoire

This is a vintage-furniture and curios store located on the hillside about a 5 minute walk from the historic center. Set in a beautiful romantic suburb, it is the ideal place to hunt for small knick-knacks, or, for those who find it feasible, classical vintage Italian furniture.

Citta del Sole

It is best to visit this store with some time in hand because of the beautiful and innovative products that are on display. This is a great place to buy gifts for children and kids. From fine handcrafted wooden toys to telescopes and barometers, the range is wide and interesting. This is part of a very popular chain which has branches all over

Italy. The store is especially crowded during the Christmas season.

Via Mazzini

This is the most popular shopping street in Verona, often referred to as the 'golden shopping mile of Verona'. It starts from the Piazza Bra and runs right up to the Piazza delle Erbe. Although there are many major global brands along the street, there are occasional smaller retailers and souvenir stores.

VERONA TRAVEL GUIDE

Know Before You Go

🌐 Entry Requirements

By virtue of the Schengen agreement, travellers from other countries in the European Union do not need a visa when visiting Italy. Additionally Swiss travellers are also exempt. Visitors from certain other countries such as the USA, Canada, Japan, Israel, Australia and New Zealand do not need visas if their stay in Italy does not exceed 90 days. When entering Italy you will be required to make a declaration of presence, either at the airport, or at a police station within eight days of arrival. This applies to visitors from other Schengen countries, as well as those visiting from non-Schengen countries.

🌐 Health Insurance

Citizens of other EU countries are covered for emergency health care in Italy. UK residents, as well as visitors from Switzerland are covered by the European Health Insurance Card (EHIC), which can be applied for free of charge. Visitors from non-Schengen countries will need to show proof of private health insurance that is valid for the duration of their stay in

Italy (that offers at least €37,500 coverage), as part of their visa application. No special vaccinations are required.

🌐 Travelling with Pets

Italy participates in the Pet Travel Scheme (PETS) which allows UK residents to travel with their pets without requiring quarantine upon re-entry. Certain conditions will need to be met. The animal will have to be microchipped and up to date on rabies vaccinations. In the case of dogs, a vaccination against canine distemper is also required by the Italian authorities. When travelling from the USA, your pet will need to be microchipped or marked with an identifying tattoo and up to date on rabies vaccinations. An EU Annex IV Veterinary Certificate for Italy will need to be issued by an accredited veterinarian. On arrival in Italy, you can apply for an EU pet passport to ease your travel in other EU countries.

🌐 Airports

Fiumicino – Leonardo da Vinci International Airport (FCO) is one of the busiest airports in Europe and the main international airport of Italy. It is located about 35km southwest of the historical quarter of Rome. Terminal 5 is used for trans-Atlantic and international flights, while Terminals 1, 2 and 3 serve mainly for domestic flights and medium haul flights to other European destinations. Before Leonardo da Vinci replaced it, the **Ciampino–G. B. Pastine International Airport** (CIA) was the main international airport servicing Rome and Italy. It is one of the oldest airports in the country still in use. Although it declined in importance, budget airlines such as Ryanair boosted its air traffic in recent years. The airport is used by Wizz Air, V Bird, Helvetic, Transavia Airlines, Sterling, Ryanair, Thomsonfly, EasyJet, Air Berlin, Hapag-Lloyd Express and Carpatair.

Milan Malpensa Airport (MXP) is the largest of the three airports serving the city of Milan. Located about 40km northwest of Milan's city center, it connects travellers to the regions of Lombardy, Piedmont and Liguria. **Milan Linate Airport** (LIN) is Milan's second international airport. **Venice Marco Polo Airport** (VCE) provides access to the charms of Venice. **Olbia Costa Smeralda Airport** (OLB) is located near Olbia, Sardinia. Main regional airports are **Guglielmo Marconi Airport** (BLQ), an international airport servicing the region of Bologna, **Capodichino Airport** at Naples (NAP), **Pisa International Airport** (PSA), formerly Galileo Galilei Airport, the main airport serving Tuscany, **Sandro Pertini Airport** near Turin (TRN), **Cristoforo Colombo** in Genoa (GOA), **Punta Raisi Airport** in Palermo (PMO), **Vincenzo Bellini Airport** in Catania (CTA) and **Palese Airport** in Bari (BRI).

VERONA TRAVEL GUIDE

🌐 Airlines

Alitalia is the flag carrier and national airline of Italy. It has a subsidiary, Alitalia CityLiner, which operates short-haul regional flights. Air Dolomiti is a regional Italian based subsidiary of of the Lufthansa Group. Meridiana is a privately owned airline based at Olbia in Sardinia.

Fiumicino - Leonardo da Vinci International Airport serves as the main hub for Alitalia, which has secondary hubs at Milan Linate and Milan Malpensa Airport. Alitalia CityLiner uses Fiumicino – Leonardo da Vinci International Airport as main hub and has secondary hubs at Milan-Linate, Naples and Trieste. Fiumicino – Leonardo da Vinci International Airport is also one of two primary hubs used by the budget Spanish airline Vueling. Milan Malpensa Airport is one of the largest bases for the British budget airline EasyJet. Venice Airport serves as an Italian base for the Spanish budget airline, Volotea, which provides connections mainly to other destinations in Europe. Olbia Costa Smeralda Airport (OLB), located near Olbia, Sardinia is the primary base of Meridiana, a private Italian Airline in partnership with Air Italia and Fly Egypt.

🌐 Currency

Italy's currency is the Euro. It is issued in notes in denominations of €500, €200, €100, €50, €20, €10 and €5.

Coins are issued in denominations of €2, €1, 50c, 20c, 10c, 5c, 2c and 1c.

🌍 Banking & ATMs

Using ATMs or Bancomats, as they are known in Italy, to withdraw money is simple if your ATM card is compatible with the MasterCard/Cirrus or Visa/Plus networks. There is a €250 limit on daily withdrawals. Italian machines are configured for 4-digit PIN numbers, although some machines will be able to handle longer PIN numbers. Bear in mind some Bancomats can run out of cash over weekends and that the more remote villages may not have adequate banking facilities so plan ahead.

🌍 Credit Cards

Credit cards are valid tender in most Italian businesses. While Visa and MasterCard are accepted universally, most tourist oriented businesses also accept American Express and Diners Club. Credit cards issued in Europe are smart cards that that are fitted with a microchip and require a PIN for each transaction. This means that a few ticket machines, self-service vendors and other businesses may not be configured to accept the older magnetic strip credit cards. Do remember to advise your bank or credit card company of your travel plans before leaving.

VERONA TRAVEL GUIDE

🌐 Tourist Taxes

Tourist tax varies from city to city, as each municipality sets its own rate. The money is collected by your accommodation and depends on the standard of accommodation. A five star establishment will levy a higher amount than a four star or three star establishment. You can expect to pay somewhere between €1 and €7 per night, with popular destinations like Rome, Venice, Milan and Florence charging a higher overall rate. In some regions, the rate is also adjusted seasonally. Children are usually exempt until at least the age of 10 and sometimes up to the age of 18. In certain areas, disabled persons and their companions also qualify for discounted rates. Tourist tax is payable directly to the hotel or guesthouse before the end of your stay.

🌐 Reclaiming VAT

If you are not from the European Union, you can claim back VAT (Value Added Tax) paid on your purchases in Italy. The VAT rate in Italy is 21 percent and this can be claimed back on your purchases if certain conditions are met. The merchant needs to be partnered with a VAT refund program. This will be indicated if the shop displays a "Tax Free" sign. The shop assistant will fill out a form for reclaiming VAT. When you submit this at the airport, you will receive your refund.

🌐 Tipping Policy

If your bill includes the phrase "coperto e servizio", that means that a service charge or tip is already included. Most waiting staff in Italy are salaried workers, but if the service is excellent, a few euros extra would be appreciated.

🌐 Mobile Phones

Most EU countries, including Italy use the GSM mobile service. This means that most UK phones and some US and Canadian phones and mobile devices will work in Italy. While you could check with your service provider about coverage before you leave, using your own service in roaming mode will involve additional costs. The alternative is to purchase an Italian SIM card to use during your stay in Italy.

Italy has four mobile networks. They are TIM, Wind, Vodafone and Tre (3) and they all provide pre-paid services. TIM offers two tourist options, both priced at €20 (+ €10 for the SIM card) with a choice of two packages - 2Gb data, plus 200 minutes call time or internet access only with a data allowance of 5Gb. Vodafone, Italy's second largest network offers a Vodafone Holiday package including SIM card for €30. They also offer the cheapest roaming rates. Wind offers an Italian Tourist pass for €20 which includes 100 minutes call time and 2Gb data and can be extended with a restart option for an extra €10.

To purchase a local SIM card, you will need to show your passport or some other form of identification and provide your residential details in Italy. By law, SIM registration is required prior to activation. Most Italian SIM cards expire after a 90 day period of inactivity. When dialling internationally, remember to use the (+) sign and the code of the country you are connecting to.

Dialling Code

The international dialling code for Italy is +39.

Emergency Numbers

Police: 113

Fire: 115

Ambulance: 118

MasterCard: 800 789 525

Visa: 800 819 014

Public Holidays

1 January: New Year's Day (Capodanno)

6 January: Day of the Epiphany (Epifania)

March-April: Easter Monday (Lunedì dell'Angelo or Pasquetta)

25 April: Liberation Day (Festa della Liberazione)

VERONA TRAVEL GUIDE

1 May: International Worker's Day (Festa del Lavoro / Festa dei Lavoratori)

2 June: Republic Day (Festa della Repubblica)

15 August: Assumption Day (Ferragosto / Assunta)

1 November: All Saints Day (Tutti i santi / Ognissanti)

8 December: Immaculate Conception (Immacolata Concezione / Immacolata)

25 December: Christmas Day (Natale)

26 December: St Stephen's Day (Santo Stefano)

A number of Saints days are observed regionally throughout the year.

Time Zone

Italy falls in the Central European Time Zone. This can be calculated as Greenwich Mean Time/Coordinated Universal Time (GMT/UTC) +2; Eastern Standard Time (North America) -6; Pacific Standard Time (North America) -9.

Daylight Savings Time

Clocks are set forward one hour on 29 March and set back one hour on 25 October for Daylight Savings Time.

🌐 School Holidays

The academic year begins in mid September and ends in mid June. The summer holiday is from mid June to mid September, although the exact times may vary according to region. There are short breaks around Christmas and New Year and also during Easter. Some regions such as Venice and Trentino have an additional break during February for the carnival season.

🌐 Trading Hours

Trading hours for the majority of shops are from 9am to 12.30pm and then again from 3.30pm to 7.30pm, although in some areas, the second shift may be from 4pm to 8pm instead. The period between 1pm and 4pm is known in Italy as the *riposo*. Large department shops and malls tend to be open from 9am to 9pm, from Monday to Saturday. Post offices are open from 8.30am to 1.30pm from Monday to Saturday. Most shops and many restaurants are closed on Sundays. Banking hours are from 8.30am to 1.30pm and then again from 3pm to 4pm, Monday to Friday. Most restaurants are open from noon till 2.30pm and then again from 7pm till 11pm or midnight, depending on the establishment. Nightclubs open around 10pm, but only liven up after midnight. Closing times vary, but will generally be between 2am and 4am. Museum hours vary, although major sights tend to be open continuously and often up to 7.30pm. Many museums are closed on Mondays.

🌍 Driving Laws

The Italians drive on the right hand side of the road. A driver's licence from any of the European Union member countries is valid in Italy. Visitors from non-EU countries will require an International Driving Permit that must remain current throughout the duration of their stay in Italy.

The speed limit on Italy's autostrade is 130km per hour and 110km per hour on main extra-urban roads, but this is reduced by 20km to 110km and 90km respectively in rainy weather. On secondary extra-urban roads, the speed limit is 90km per hour; on urban highways, it is 70km per hour and on urban roads, the speed limit is 50km per hour. You are not allowed to drive in the ZTL or Limited Traffic Zone (or *zona traffico limitato* in Italian) unless you have a special permit.

Visitors to Italy are allowed to drive their own non-Italian vehicles in the country for a period of up to six months. After this, they will be required to obtain Italian registration with Italian licence plates. Italy has very strict laws against driving under the influence of alcohol. The blood alcohol limit is 0.05 and drivers caught above the limit face penalties such as fines of up to €6000, confiscation of their vehicles, suspension of their licenses and imprisonment of up to 6 months. Breathalyzer tests are routine at accident scenes.

🌐 Drinking Laws

The legal drinking age in Italy is 16. While drinking in public spaces is allowed, public drunkenness is not tolerated. Alcohol is sold in bars, wine shops, liquor stores and grocery shops.

🌐 Smoking Laws

In 2005, Italy implemented a policy banning smoking from public places such as bars, restaurants, nightclubs and working places, limiting it to specially designated smoking rooms. Further legislation banning smoking from parks, beaches and stadiums is being explored.

🌐 Electricity

Electricity: 220 volts

Frequency: 50 Hz

Italian electricity sockets are compatible with the Type L plugs, a plug that features three round pins or prongs, arranged in a straight line. An alternate is the two-pronged Type C Euro adaptor. If travelling from the USA, you will need a power converter or transformer to convert the voltage from 220 to 110, to avoid damage to your appliances. The latest models of many laptops, camcorders, mobile phones and digital cameras are dual-voltage with a built in converter.

🌐 Tourist Information (TI)

There are tourist information (TI) desks at each of the terminals of the Leonardo da Vinci International Airport, as well as interactive Information kiosks with the latest touch-screen technology. In Rome, the tourist office can be found at 5 Via Parigi, near the Termini Station and it is identified as APT, which stands for Azienda provinciale del Turismo. Free maps and brochures of current events are available from tourist kiosks.

Several of the more tourist-oriented regions of Italy offer tourist cards that include admission to most of the city's attractions. While these cards are not free, some offer great value for money. A variety of tourism apps are also available online.

🌐 Food & Drink

Pasta is a central element of many typically Italian dishes, but there are regional varieties and different types of pasta are matched to different sauces. Well known pasta dishes such as lasagne and bolognaise originated in Bologna. Stuffed pasta is popular in the northern part of Italy, while the abundance of seafood and olives influences southern Italian cuisine. As far as pizza goes, the Italians differentiate between the thicker Neapolitan pizza and the thin crust Roman pizza, as well as white pizza, also known as focaccia and tomato based pizza. Other standards include minestrone soup, risotto, polenta and a variety of cheeses, hams, sausages and salamis. If you are on a budget, consider snacking on stuzzichini with a few drinks during happy hour which is often between 7 and 9pm. The fare can include salami, cheeses, cured meat, mini pizzas, bread, vegetables, pastries or pate. In Italy, Parmesan refers only to cheese originating from the area surrounding Parma. Favorites desserts include tiramisu or Italian gelato.

Italians enjoy relaxing to aperitifs before they settle down to a meal and their favorites are Campari, Aperol or Negroni, the famous Italian cocktail. Wine is enjoyed with dinner. Italy is particularly famous for its red wines. The best known wine regions are Piedmont, which produces robust and dry reds, Tuscany and Alto Adige, where Alpine soil adds a distinctive acidity. After the meal, they settle down to a glass of limoncello, the country's most popular liqueur, or grappa, which is distilled from grape seeds and stems, as digestive. Other options in this class include a nut liqueur, nocino, strawberry based Fragolino Veneto or herbal digestives like gineprino, laurino or mirto. Italians are also fond of coffee. Espresso is drunk through throughout the day, but cappuccino is considered a morning drink. The most popular beers in Italy are Peroni and Moretti.

🌐 Websites

http://vistoperitalia.esteri.it/home/en

This is the website of the Consulate General of Italy. Here you can look up whether you will need a visa and also process your application online.

http://www.italia.it/en/home.html

The official website of Italian tourism

http://www.italia.it/en/useful-info/mobile-apps.html

Select the region of your choice to download a useful mobile app to your phone.

http://www.italylogue.com/tourism

http://italiantourism.com/index.html

http://www.reidsitaly.com/

http://wikitravel.org/en/Italy

https://www.summerinitaly.com/

http://www.accessibleitalianholiday.com/

Planning Italian vacations around the needs of disabled tourists.